SONGS OF THE MIND'S MIND

(POEMS)

John Ngong Kum Ngong

Miraclaire Publishing
Kansas City, (MO)

MIRACLAIRE PUBLISHING LLC
Kansas City, (MO) USA

Website: *www.miraclairepublishing.com*
Email: *info@miraclairepublishing.com*

ISBN-13: 978-0615957708
ISBN-10: 0615957706

All rights reserved.
No part of this publication may be reproduced by any means, graphic, electronic, or mechanical, including photocopying, recording, taping or by any information storage retrieval system without the prior written permission of the copyright holder, except in the case of brief quotations embodied in critical articles and reviews.

© 2014 Miraclaire Publishing
John Ngong Kum Ngong

Printed in the United States of America

Miraclaire Publishing makes every effort to ensure the accuracy of all the information ("Content") in its publications. However, Miraclaire and its agents and licensors make no representations or warranties whatsoever as to the accuracy, completeness, or suitability for any purpose of the Content and disclaim all such representations and warranties, whether expressed or implied to the maximum extent permitted by law. Any views expressed in this publication are the views of the author and are not necessarily the views of Miraclaire.

Contents

WET NEIGHBOUR 5
SOMEDAY SOMEONE WILL UNDERSTAND 7
IGNORANT SULLEN SOULS 9
LOOK OVER YOUR SHOULDER 11
MIND IN FINE FETTLE 13
THE KEY 15
MEDDLING MIND 17
TRAIL THE RAYS 19
TIMES THAT USED TO BE 21
ONE DREAM ONE AMBITION 23
TEARS AND PRAYER 25
VIPERS IN THE BOSOM 27
SATISFACTION 29
WHEN FIRST I BEHELD YOU 31
STUNNING BEAUTY 33
SEASONING SOULMATE 35
BEAUTY IS SHORT-LIVED 37
WOULD I WERE LIKE YOU 39
NEW-FOUND LOVE I 41
NEW-FOUND LOVE II 43
NEW-FOUND LOVE 111 45
SING WITH ME 47
CREEP UP ON ME 49
THE PROMISE 51
AMAZING OFFER 53
LAY YOUR HEART ON MY BREAST 55
DESTINY 57
WE CAN 59
WAITING 1 61
WAITING 11 63
COVERED WITH GUILT 65

BRAVE BREAST	67
COUNTING ON YOU 1	69
COUNTING ON YOU 11	70
OVERLOADED HEART	72
DEEP CARE	74
FUWAM THE PROFESSOR 1	76
FUWAM THE PROFESSOR 11	77
FUWAM THE PROFESSOR 111	79
LITTLE UFONG 1	81
LITTLE UFONG 11	83
TAKE BACK YOUR LOVE	85
TREACHEROUS ARROW	87
EARNEST APPEAL	89
I LOVE WHISTLING	91
BREATHING STILL	93
STILL SMALL VOICE	95
THEY WILL RISE	97
FIND YOUR FEET AGAIN	99
BEYOND BELIEF	101
KATAKATA	103
TURN LOOSE THE BEAST	106
INTRANSIGENT FISTS	108
DANCE OF THE END	110

WET NEIGHBOUR

I know Fayah Sanseiyah
my wet but gentle neighbour
who for many years has borne
the teeth of cold-blooded care
and the genocidal tongue
of rebuff and rejection.
I must admit careworn folk
that never before but now
have I thought profoundly of
the terror, the deep dark nights
he spends in ash and sackcloth
writhing in the glare of scorn.
I must admit dear reader
that never before this day
have I felt with such trembling
the thorny fingers of fear
the cold hands of indifference
and the heavy rain of blows
fascist dry-eyed Ignorance
rains on Fayah Sanseiyah.

I know Fayah Sanseiyah well
the neighbour who agreed to draw
the blood of bloody Ignorance
and break loose like a savaged steed
from the barbed-wire fence of shame.
I know you would be scared to death
and burden me with reproaches
instead of bursting into song

to warm Fayah Sanseiyah's heart
and show him the way to survive.
I know you will try to escape
carrying along your old drums
ready to barter your conscience
and sing subservient songs to live
ignorant of your people's ways.
The jaws of Ignorance and Fear
will certainly crush you to death
save you strip Cowardice of brawn.
Only then will you be able
to see and appreciate the world

SOMEDAY SOMEONE WILL UNDERSTAND

My dear countrymen
wet behind the ears,
dying to dine well.
Make eyes with sound songs
shifting stirring songs,
songs of the mind's mind,
songs that call to mind
scenes that dog our steps
and blow ablaze the flames,
the fire in my heart,
the passion to spin songs
to match the rocky road
we have trod night and day.
Someday somehow, someone
will understand our case
and give Justice love bites.
We must sport confidence
at the ready to crow.

My mind likes mining for
songs that cudgel the mind
and trigger off the heart,
songs that war against self
to inject life into
the dying, the swindled.
Hold hands with such soft songs
dear fellow countrymen
when the body nods off
and the heart is unnerved.

I have no more tears mates
to spill for feeble flesh
unable to stand straight
to strip fools bare of life.
I have tear-jerking songs
mixed and matched with frank love,
search songs of the mind's mind
for souls soaked in sorrow,
souls struggling to break free
from crippling ignorance,
souls that do not feel loved
like Fayah Sanseiyah.

IGNORANT SULLEN SOULS

I know you have seen
souls sullen and slim
sitting on their hands
like Fayah Sanseiyah.
I know you do not know
they do not know themselves.
They have never, since birth
shaken hands with fat cats
let alone get wind of
the fragrance of true love.
They have never thought of
the beauty of plain truth
nor the wrinkles of masks.
The foul face of hunger
and the dim eyes of thirst
know that such sombre souls
are ignorant and dead
so they push them around
like toys and chess pieces
into the jaws of puff adders.

Now that your heart sees red
and your mind ticks with zeal,
I know wrath will rock you
like a boat in the storm
till you make up your mind
to cross swords with hitmen.
I know the voice of Love
will go down on her knees

to make you get to know
the dogs spreading terror
and the ignorant souls
writhing in mud like worms.
I wish you could pull tight
around the neck of fear
the noose of the hangman
and pick the road to school.
I wish you could learn fast
to whet our people's minds
to dance the kind of dance
we danced before invaders came.

LOOK OVER YOUR SHOULDER

Ignorance is a harsh master
mangling those beholden to him.
I have seen you recoil often
lowbrow brother clung to custom,
clutching your stomach like a kid
struggling to fight off barbed hunger.
I feel your anguish in my bones
and wish you were knowledgeable.
Implore your mind to browse with you
when the steel fingers of blue funk
tighten their grip on your sore throat.

Look over your shoulder thickhead
before mental darkness swamps you.
I have never settled my mind
on shortening the limbs of hope
nor vows exchanged with dejection.
I want to see you grow up bloke
into a man of sound standards
to grow love in our people's hearts.
I see courage in your keen eyes
but panic twists your muscled arms.
Invite your mind to fight with you
when your emotions betray you.

I will give my eyeteeth for you
on my knees daylong in my heart
to cover our shame with your head.
Look over your shoulder greenhorn

before the world creeps into you.
Do not go crazy over life
but worm yourself into shelter
before the world devastates you
and worms eat to their hearts' content.
I see fortitude on your face.
Entreat your mind to march with you
when your companions let you down.

Ignorance is a vile spirit
sucking the blood of lazy minds.
I have seen you dizzy sometimes
over the missiles in our hearts.
Let the fleas in your ignorance
not drain the blood in your bosom.
I have longed to lead you away
from the path that will destroy you.
Light a fire to burn your shame
and savage the beast in my heart.
Cry out to your mind for wisdom
when the sky refuses to weep.

MIND IN FINE FETTLE

A mind in fine fettle
has eyes sound as a bell.
It peers into the past,
keeps in sight the present
and peeps at the future
to live a worthwhile life,
a life straight and immersed
in songs of the mind's mind,
songs that give root to dreams
even to living souls
living on borrowed time.

I have a mind with eyes
astute and large as life.
It roams about sometimes,
holds in view present time
and sports with bygone days
to stand tall the morrow
regardless of my age.
Sometimes it calls to mind
things foul and things pleasant.
There are times as well when
it dreams sounding brass dreams,
drums up rage with great skill
and paints hair-raising scenes
that torment weak-kneed minds.

I cherish the songs I hear
saucy songs of the mind's mind

in contempt of my age.
They dare one to have in mind
not just the world close to one
but the death of truth as well
and the dearth of genuine love.
So a mind in fine fettle
has eyes that see everything.
It broods over the present,
angles for what used to be
and craves to grasp the future
to compose songs that provoke,
searching songs of the mind's mind.

THE KEY

Minds dull as ditch water
drive me crazy sometimes
so I must seek once more
the help of my weird mind.
It sees things underground
and gets furious with dimwits
but not with me, key of hope.

My mind sometimes perceives
what my eyes cannot see.
At such moments I stoop
and let it throw its spear
at those who slay to shine.
I stretch my love beyond
the reach of mindless pain
so I should not weep again
for I am the key to fame.

It is my duty to paint well
the pictures whether good or bad,
and the scenes, whether dull or bright
from my mind's progressive lenses.
I am the hammer and the nail,
the only servant and the key
my mind usually makes use of
when unable to find answers
to the dilemma of our past.
We are ready for great battles
my mind and I before the sun,

for our people to wail no more.
I am willing to strip strangers
for my people to beg no more.
I am the servant and the key
to unlock the door to conquest.

MEDDLING MIND

I have a meddling mind
that skips from love to tears
and peeps into grown gloom,
the shaded side of life
hopeful, somehow hopeful
that it will make people
see the scruffiness it sees.

I have a crazy mind
that mounts mountainous zones
and flies from trees to homes,
the sacred points of love
hopeful, somehow hopeful
that it will make lovers
see the beauty it sees.
It believes no person,
save one with its genius
can understand its thoughts
and love what it presents.
I will mine with my weird mind.

My queer mind knows the world
will laugh when it descends
like a kite shot in space.
I am convinced my friends
with minds endowed with eyes
except they be bewitched
will harass hearts with calls,
calls that cannot be stopped,

calls that you cannot kill
or turn a blind eye to,
calls that build a people.
I will die with my queer mind.

I will sing the mind of mind
till the harvest of my heart
fills the trays in my love's heart.
I will paint what my mind sees
and trespass on your feelings
singing till I lose my voice.
I will rise with my quaint mind.

TRAIL THE RAYS

My mind mindful is out of gear,
my eyes man-size on the lookout
rake through broken revolting streets,
nursing hope to find fulfilment.
My vital fluid hot as pepper
surges through my nail-biting veins
like water from an unloosed dam.
Love can drive someone delirious
save the sun and moon intervene
and the rays of the sun confirm.

Don't sorrow for me dear friends
at a time like this, parched time
when the land hangs upside down.
Don't assign trust to your tongues
pregnant with white lies and death.
Give a chance to your intellect
and pay attention to conscience
to feel the pulse of genuine love.
Give a chance to the burdened heart
and take heed of the crestfallen
to comprehend the strains of want.
You think too little slack comrades
and babble too much like babies.
Losing out to hatred breaks dawn
and sets free the imprisoned soul.

Your praise singing is without tears,
your love barren as a desert.

You have drawn a scarlet curtain
over the sludge in your backyard
and given the world wrong signals.
Trail the rays of the rising sun
before the savage storm I sniff
rips open your stinking stomach.
Trail the rays of the rising sun
before the twine of doom ropes you.

TIMES THAT USED TO BE

I love you all soulmates
in no mood to sing trash.
I see guts in your eyes
all set for a choice song
for times that used to be,
times when we loved like doves
flying from place to place
free from slaps in the face.
Such were the times soulmates
with their flaws, pangs and grief
but times when love was love.
They were times without strain,
times when we worked like ants
to save for grey times in time.
Such times now turn in the grave
with no songs to sing their minds.

I salute you hearts of oak
disposed to pen searching songs
for times like these without eyes,
times when Love and Truth posture
like strangers in their own home
munching in silence stale crumbs.
Such are the times countrymen
with their sores, coldness and heat,
times when everyone trades love
to have a down on justice.
They are times fraught with danger,
times when you should not bed down

without sticking in your mind
the sketch of the state you want.
I salute you soul brothers
struggling hard to make us seen.

I espy green light near the hills
and children lighting up the land
with lamps of love and rectitude
reflecting times that used to be,
times when we lived like companions
hugging each other everyday.
They were times without deadly doubt,
times when each hale and hearty mind
leapt to the support of the poor,
ready to bleed for their rights too.
Such times are rotting in the grave
with no mouths to vaunt their exploits.
These days every man and woman
wants his or her name to figure
in the list of record breakers
milking the land for their profits.

ONE DREAM ONE AMBITION

Return beguiling lady
to the tests of yesterday
when perplexing destiny
decked in hysterical dreams
drove me into your green grounds
where stumbling on winsome blooms
I sprawled on them roused to life.

Return intriguing woman
to the tests of yesterday
when like a suckling tigress
you tore into the garden
set to tear me into bits.
I saw anger in your eyes
and fear, not right in the head
like the slash of a new knife,
cut open wounds of neglect.
Frightful ooze dripped from my sides
and flowed freely down the lane
leading to where your heart slept.

Return bewitching lady
to the tests of yesterday
when uncompromising fate
dressed in down to earth outfit,
drew me to shake hands with you
when the sun slid down the hills.
I screamed struck by your beauty.

Moved, you made a move towards me
terrified in your brand-new shoes.
The sun wholehearted as usual
was sliding down behind the hills
smiling, pleased to see us so close.
I never knew you could wriggle
under the lash of scalding eyes
in the heat of opposing thoughts.
I still remember the moments
spent on the ground, turning over
in my mind, the naked truth that
we share one dream, one ambition.

TEARS AND PRAYER

See how I burn out
worn out by the search
for earnest soulmates.
I know you will snub me
to win the hearts of sharks
deaf to our cry for light.
I hear, through the grapevine
you love the shameful role
bitches have assigned you,
an ass standing their strain.
I weep for you blind friend
though my mind fights for you.

Politicians and dopes
will not understand me
nor love what I proclaim,
the self-esteem of man.
I never pressed a suit
to be born in this place
where people fear daylight.
They make love to darkness
and close the door to thought
to blot out love and truth.
I weep for you dear folk
and pray your minds should tick.

Scholars and theorists
will strip me naked
in foul-smelling bars

and rowdy lecture rooms.
I never wished to play
the complicated role
fate set aside for me,
an artist churning out
songs screaming at Abuse.
I never wished to swim
against the strong current
of the state's deep river
flowing fast and furious
till eagles drew my blood
and murdered love and truth.
I weep for you scorched land
and pray the rains kiss you.
I weep for you silent souls
and pray the seasons heal you
before the fight of the end.

VIPERS IN THE BOSOM

When like termites in flight
after sharp sheets of rain
you and I, starved with cold
crawled home to heat our souls,
our hearts in our cracked mouths
some folk threw stones at us.
No friend let a tear fall
nor called across the storm
to still the pain we felt.
Only our minds bore the brunt.

Vipers in the bosom
advised you to leave me
to turn the key on you.
I will neither nail them
nor run down their titles.
I will suffer them sing
anytime, their misdeeds
till the winds make them plain.
The tried sun will teach me
to face life like a knight
bold, ready and willing to
put heart into tortured souls.
You too can tutor your mind
to blow to bits the vipers.

Vipers in the bosom
spread tall tales about me
to seal your fate in stain.

I will neither shame them
nor nurse hate against them.
I will suffer them weigh
any time, their mischief
till time brings them to light.
The mild moon will show me
the way to shine like stars
fair, ready and willing to
crush vipers in the bosom.
You too can plead with the sun
to scorch their minds and spirits.

SATISFACTION

Peeping back in time,
I see my mum miffed
yanking my small ears
to straighten my life.
I see her bent double,
holding her head in pain
near some dying embers.
I think the world of her
though she no longer breathes.
The warmth I used to feel
on her laps warms my heart
and my mind leaps in joy.

Stumbling along life
in the crack of dawn
as well as nightfall,
in darksome areas
as well as shining ones,
I came across a heart
gentle and full of grace,
unlike the ones I knew
violent and void of shame.
He drove me to a park
with various kinds of bloom,
his mind full of fair songs.

I stared at the flowers,
bent down with extreme care
and plucked a purple rose

undried, and have kept it
not only in my room
but in my heart also.
I know mum is happy
and the sun, red like blood
descending behind the hills
surrounding my plain homestead,
is satisfied and glad too.
My fair purple Rose and I
above the noise of bad vibes
are also over the moon.
We are easy in our minds
and love to hate hypocrites.
We are more than satisfied
with the beams in our wedlock
though jealous hearts go all out
to tarnish our household name.

WHEN FIRST I BEHELD YOU

The day was bright and lovely
without a cloud in the sky
when I first beheld you dear.
I studied your sunlit face,
the seasoning in your eyes
the polish in your laughter
the buttermilk in your voice
and convinced my canny heart
to explore the winding route
leading to your harried heart.

The wild instincts of the beast
surged out from the subconscience
swollen with blinkered passion
sure as death and free as air,
determined to knock you flat.
I started a great field trip
from inside, holding my breath,
dumbstruck by your sheer beauty.
The day was bright and lovely
and weaver birds had a ball.

The day was fresh and friendly
without a cloud in the sky.
I felt the heart of the ground
beating faster, flushed with rage
dressed to prick my cheeky soles
to make me eat humble pie.
The fear of failure, the scourge

made me start at my own shadow.
I managed to raise high my head
confident my dream would flower.

STUNNING BEAUTY

I have never seen such beauty,
blinding beauty snaring beauty
enveloped in a lone creature,
laying bare the fangs of thousands
dying inthe attempt to mount
the horse Venus often wears out.
I mounted it when I was young
but failed to arrive my station.
You too can bend over backwards
to sound the grandeur of Beauty.

After many seasons of toil
deaf to swirling opposition,
I broke the spirit of the horse
and stretched myself out upon it,
well prepared to kiss Beauty's hands
floating along with her calm flow.
It was such a hair-raising chance
I could hardly have forty winks.
Then in the twinkling of an eye
you turned green with envy Fuwam.
With one hand tied behind your back
you slid into shameless contracts
willing to dash your people's charms
against saw-edged cliffs of terror.
You knocked me down with a feather
but I slew surprise and drudged on.

I have never seen such beauty

smashing beauty catching beauty
wrapped around a single creature,
taking the wraps off so many souls
striving without success to ride
the stallion Beauty often mounts.
You can mount it and ride away
Fuwam, to the place of your heart
provided you paddle upstream
ready to die with your boots on.

SEASONING SOULMATE

Look at her trim figure
and gentle eyes of blue.
They are lovely to behold
under the sway of cloud nine.
Just lay your eyes on her laps
smooth as glass and goddesslike
regardless of her middle life.

Look at Wiyam my love
my seasoning soulmate,
the woman of my bosom.
Mark the polish in her gait
mouthwatering and graceful,
the measured steps of beauty.
I offer her my conquered heart.

Take Beauty in your hands
to deal with the Ugly,
observing life like a hawk
roosting in a skyhigh tree,
working out its next victim.
Beauty gives suck to the heart
and makes man mouth desire.
I think the world of my love,
my true to the core princess.
I will always bang the drum
and keep faith with my conscience
in the presence of your blood.
I will sound your horn everywhere

in the daytime and the night-time
in the deep entrails of the land
till the Grim Reaper comes for me.

BEAUTY IS SHORT-LIVED

Iwa, clean-limbed lady
from the heart of the hills
fresh as the morning sun.
I love to watch you walk
resplendent, natural woman.
Beauty is like a rose abloom
pretty woman of the hills.
It flourishes like all flowers
ensnares butterflies and then fades
like a garment not well tinctured.

Like a daisy in full bloom
luring moths and honeybees
in the early morning sun,
many people gaze on you
thinking you are a honeypot.
Assailed with flattery and notes
you spare them space in your garden
and endorse their ruthless requests
to suck your nectar without break.
I swell with fury young lady.

Lovely woman of the hills,
when the magic in your steps
and the perfume in your voice,
when the lustre in your eyes
and the charm you wear depreciate,
they will desert you high and dry.
When wrinkles overrun your face

the villains will walk out on you.
Then like a rotten pawpaw fruit
you will fall with no tried voices
to sing your eye-popping beauty
nor tears to mitigate your end.
Lovely lady of the high hills
beauty is like break of day dew
sparkling like silver but short-lived.

WOULD I WERE LIKE YOU

Would I were like you woman,
not in beauty facing death
nor ugliness watching dumb
the last nails being driven
into the forehead of Love,
I would take aim at the stars,
spread my hands towards the sun
and ask for love and music.

Would I were like you woman,
locked in the palace of self
selling to a blighted world
hope that on no occasion
would drive people to the hills
to view the world differently,
I would take leave of my wits
to shoot my love in the eyes.

Would I were like you woman,
I would ask other women
like you to gather with me
to silence lame Love and live.
I want freedom in my love
and poems that remind the lame
to resist the blows of fate.
I want them to understand
the world lames many people
and chews the hearts of cowards.
I want them to know that though

the world lets loose tyranny
and breaks the teeth of nigglers,
I hobble and cry with them.
I cannot put up for sale
my soul for the world to live.
Would I were like you lady,
I would trap the morning sun
and tread on the hills of fact,
draped like a sewing woman.

NEW-FOUND LOVE I

Kisses rollick on my lips
whenever I think of you.
A winsome word from you would
nodules in my heart squeeze dry.
See how I take sick for you
unable to chew choice food.
How I wish love coupled us
ending years of skirmishes
kicking the ribs of rebuff.
Egg me on to keep dreaming
if our venture must bear fruit.

Embark with me new-found love
under the eyes of the crowd.
News of our romance has spread
igniting grim thoughts in hearts
clamouring still for your heart
eating already from my dish.

Knock the wind out of rascals
whenever they come for you.
Allow no fortune-hunter
near the kernel of our tryst.
See how I swim after you
unable to think rightly.
How I wish love knotted us
ending years of haunting fear
keeping me from your embrace.
Ease my way through obstacles

if our endeavour must thrive.

Enter with me new-found love
undisguised, into our grounds.
News of our friendship has spread
igniting rage in peers still
clamouring for your fair heart
eager to share my close dreams.

NEW-FOUND LOVE II

Kisses still dance on my lips
whenever my eyes meet yours
and my heart billows in joy.
No daft dare come between us
save Death, the subtle Serpent.
Underneath your heart lies love
humble, bubbling with keen care
even when I slash your breast
kneeling in front of my psyche.
Enhance my knowledge of love
if our union must brave time.

Encase my slips new-found love
under the tree of your breast.
No flesh I think will drag us
into the arms of dry bones
clinging still to their dream of
edging their way through our hearts.

Keep at bay conscience killers
whenever you think of me.
Admit no unknown persons
nor friends thirsty like deserts.
Show the world your gravitas
unbroken and trustworthy,
honest sand steaming with love
even when the sky is grey
kissing the sun in darkness.
Exert pressure on ill will

if our wedlock must survive.

Entrust me with your warm heart
under the eyes of sworn foes.
Nothing but plots will push us
into the dark room of guile
clutching still its mad dream of
emerging tall in our hearts.

NEW-FOUND LOVE 111

The beauty I beheld
burning bright in your eyes
bid me sow seeds of love
on the soil of your soul.
They sprouted in season
and have borne oranges
that make me sing better.

I now know you so well
like the teeth in my mouth
and can lay down my head
on the laps of your breasts
in and out of season.
The lone road to my heart
where doubt and fear once crawled
and foes fought hard to block
stands clear and clean today.

You can walk tall on it,
the lone road to my love
that skirts a small rose bed
and leads to the town square
where I used to stand still
watching you play with friends.
I know you know I knew
the track you always took
when the sun bottomed out
but you could not see well
the knight waiting for you.

I now know you so well
like the hair on my head
and can lay down my life
for you at any cost.
I now feel much better
with you always with me
my black and blue goddess.
I cannot be so daft
to ditch such new-found love
for the faint face of fame.
I will kiss and curdle
your gift of endearment
and love like an angel.

SING WITH ME

Sing with me dearest friend,
the pink cheeks of the sun
and the sweet smell of blooms.
Sing with me fairest friend
till the mouths close by us
sing against greed and guile.
Each time I bring to mind
the raw courage of youth
lost in the wilds of ripeness,
my heart pales like the wan moon.

Sing with me bosom friend,
the good cheer of the moon
and the foul smell of rats.
Sing with me seemly match
till the craftsmen near us
see the need to carve Truth.
When sanguinely I brood
over the claws of clods
grown in the woods of wreck,
    my mind spins like a drunk's.
Draw near sensational friend
so we can sing seasoned songs
that gather every sound soul
in the grounds of agreement
before hawks come down on us.
Draw near creditable friend
so we can bring forth music
that brings together able heads

in the field of inventiveness
before sham singers gain more ground.

CREEP UP ON ME

Creep up on me my love
so I can sing in depth
for souls that burn to love.
Come closer my sweetheart
so we can warm our hearts.
It is too cold these days.
The dainty deal we struck
years back with distant bards
has grown razor-sharp teeth,
slashing the tongue of Truth.

Come then my pretty bright mate
so we can dance with finesse
the dance of our flesh and blood.
It used to make my blood rise
but now its rhythm is bland.
Come dear woman of my youth
so we can teach our children
the dance that used to make us
shoot up skyward like eagles
but now its spirit stands doomed.

Creep up on me my dear
so we can like parrots
parrot the lack of love
and pull the ears of lies,
of gossip and falsehood
that turn couples to beasts.
Come apple of my eye

so we can make crowds dream
and stop bellicose sprites
from singing songs of doom.
Come that like an eagle
we may glide through the sky
and swoop down on fake poets
looters of the state
whose deeds belie their words.

THE PROMISE

I know I ran through your heart
and left you out in the cold
when life's incisors sank deep
into my sore and frail flesh.
I could bear neither your tears
nor watch you go to pieces.
I was not out to wound you
or break the legs of your mind
to dress the wounds in my heart.

I knew you were going to cry
from break of day to sundown
not because you had read me
but because I had dressed you
like a queen amidst loose eyes.
I did not mean to grieve you
or paint you black in public.
I was out to guard your charm
and balloon your mind with love.

I will spread your probity
like a straw mat in public
for every thoughtful writer
to lie on and spin love songs.
I will leaf through you daily
and sing about your promise
to battle to gain new grounds
and set alight fresh fire
to char Discord and Disdain.

Let vultures pick at my eyes
and worms polish off my brains
if I feed your flames with lies.
I promise with all my heart
to seat you close to my heart
even when the world shoots me.
I promise to prune your views
and turn upside down with care
the room to father our dreams.

AMAZING OFFER

Leave your steaming rage princess
tainted on my threadbare mat.
Crooks and hirelings nose around
seeking to stain the beauty
heaven has endowed you with.
Dirty dogs and hearts of gold
breeze past daily where you live
hoping to slake their passions.

I offer you my mat dear
my breast and my feelings too
wrapped in our people's customs.
Let them your companions be
in both light and pitch darkness.
I offer you my dear life
wrapped in fresh cocoyam leaves.
Let it throw light on our love.

Leave your piercing emotions
and the teardrops in your voice
near the sweepings by the road.
I have cleared the junk inside
and left water in a dish
for your face and dusty feet.
You are the flower I need,
the bee to make me honey.

I offer you my mad heart,
my hands and my mind also

soaked in our people's wisdom.
Let them your new actors be
in both the day and the night.
I offer you all my love
wrapped in sacrificial cloth.
Let it thrust you to the top.

LAY YOUR HEART ON MY BREAST

I remember still my dear
when evening's light faded
and the day crawled away faint
how I crept into my mind
and gave thought the whole night
to what tomorrow will bring.
I was really scared to death
till you lay your soothing heart
on my breast trembling with fear.

I remember still my love
how often I searched for you
in the day, in the night tense,
to empty my mind to you.
I wanted to tell you dear
to lay not your heart on earth
nor on the laps of born fools.
I could not stand the blood and tears
of maids with broken limbs and spines
so lay not your heart on shadows
nor on the laps of criminals.
I cannot stand the rape and blood
of lasses with no tomorrow
so lay not your heart on conmen
nor on the oath of cabbalists.

Lay your hot heart on my breast
to shame the people who see
but wreck in the rays of light

letting off steam in our eyes.
Genuine love you may doubt it,
still exists, even in name.
It can give meaning to life,
keep one's nose to the grindstone
and seed the seeds of fairness.

DESTINY

I saw you wrapped in thought
and my heart bled in tears.
It cut through and through faint,
watching you sigh ceaselessly
in silence like a shadow.
The urge to swoop down on you
like a hawk ready to kill,
swept through me like a whirlwind.
I waited for the right time
to drive my keen knife into
the stinking belly of fear.

I swerved to you sweating
and held out my right hand,
cheerful though stabbed by doubt.
Your eyes, quickened with sorrow,
convinced me to lay my heart
on the laps of your headache.
The grief in your eyes narrowed,
your face flooded with sunbeams
and then you burst out laughing.
I carried you like an egg
away from sharks and humbug.
Destiny brought us together
and enabled us to tie the knot.

If this be the birth of joy
in the labour room of pain
then let me no longer roam

nor lament the loss of self.
Let me wear the hat of charm
with lovesick strains for your ears
my love, in darkness and light
in the groove of gracefulness.
If this be the sauce of love
then let me no longer stew
nor drink the soup of bitches.
Let me live life to the full
with your sixth sense on my breast
my love, for better or for worse
in the belly of life to come.

WE CAN

I know that I am dust
even as you too are
bound to be blown away
someday like paltry chaff.
We can rise tough woman
above the dust and live.
Many people won't understand
why we reason the way we do
daylong to steer clear of conflicts.
Many more believe we are mad
moaning the death of plain speaking.
I believe the swift tide of love
stirring in the heart of our hearts
can stir the minds of our people
to shatter the stones in their hearts
and flush distrust out of their blood.

I know that Love's sly eyes
seek but men with gold mines
even as her deceitful tongue
lures simpletons into their graves.
We can show this moronic world
how to love without deception.
We can light fires fair woman
in the hearts of dying persons
to revive their once buoyant guts.
We can prepare the way today
for those who tomorrow would love
to love and be attached to love

coining songs with frenetic beats
to beat sense into our people.
I believe no human muscle
would wrest us from passion's clutches.
You and I can strengthen my mind
to pipe songs for bedridden minds.

WAITING 1

Sleep the sleep of the fair
in your soft bed of blooms
sweet dame of the season.
Let not my naughty notes
soil your thoughts in the train
your mind has just boarded.
I wait to embrace you
cute woman of my heart
when you get off that train.
I yearn to welcome you
humming hymns with my mind
in my modest workshop
so dreary without you.

Thin on the ground lady
out of line in pale green
yet bright and beautiful.
Do not allow false friends,
wolves wearing white garments
deceive you with their smiles.
They put up for sale death
wrapped in red handkerchiefs.
I thirst for you in truth
and moon after sound love
and the nurse in your heart.
I wait to do you proud
singing loud in my mind.

Go on sleeping woman.

Sleep the sleep of the clean
in your coach of comfort.
People may jump and dance
on both sides of your heart
but do not let them steal
the flame that keeps me warm.
Do not give hope to quacks,
hands that refuse to raise
decent homes for the blind.
You are worth a king's raid.
I wait to take you in
dancing gay in my mind.

WAITING 11

The moon is full tonight
sleek and free and easy
like a plum tree in bloom.
Owls have gathered hungry
on the tree in your yard.
They have chosen your home
for their next sacrifice.
Can you not hear my love
the bang in their laughter
that will end in slaughter
unless you use your mind?

Alone you feel hot breeze
blow across your forehead
but the owls laugh at you.
Alone you think of death
provoked by doubt and shame
but the owls jump for joy.
Can you not see my dear
the plot in their actions
and the beast in their eyes
that will butcher your dreams
unless you rouse your mind?

The moon is full tonight
for you and I to meet.
She wants to chat with us
the moon, bright and lovely.
The woman in your eyes

rolling stripped in the dust
numb with fear, wants to frisk.
Come, for the moon is full tonight
ready to beat the drum of love.
I wait burning before your door
my heart and my mind in combat.

The owls sigh in disgust
not of the mind to mind
the music from our hearts.
We wait, the moon and I.
You cannot thrive in gloom
nor rise above foul tongues
without the prop of friends.
We wait, the moon and your Romeo
prepared to throw you a lifeline.
I cannot leave you in the lurch
even when my mind sings sad songs.

COVERED WITH GUILT

In the heart of the dry season
when dust promises hell to all,
my partner and I come to grips.
She says I never should doubt her
even when heat threatens measles
and tongues fabricate bogus proofs
but being shifty I would shout
and shend my beloved for treason.

When the rains rush in in torrents
washing off some dreams we have nursed
my helpmeet goes down on her knees.
She says I never should cheat her
even when coldness freezes me
and strumpets promise me silver
but being canny I would curse
and push around the train of thought.

At twilight as we watch the sun
glide down the hills in resplendence
my mate demands I stroll with her
as the sun wakes and sleeps daily
but being tense I would split hairs,
challenge her to assault her mind
and stitch up the wound in my heart.
She pleads with me throughout the night
to understand her but I rave
only to be covered with guilt.

Now I perceive very clearly
the affection that often dances
rapturous in her catlike eyes.
Now I know devotion makes good
and attention cements the mind
to hold out against love's outrage.
Forebearance I have also learnt
and believe love can bar bloodshed
and give adolescents the chance
to beat their breasts in market squares.

BRAVE BREAST

I will shelter you well
deep down my interior
and go on bended knee
to implore nature's boost.
I will erect your front
in front of my dwelling
and think of it always
till my vital spark dies.
Hang my love on your neck
and think always of our vows.

I know green-eyed people
would think am eccentric
raising high mankind's fall.
They fought to crown you queen
but since none in their midst
could belt out your fragrance
nor sing of your bright eyes,
they failed to stay the course.
My love spear pierced your heart
and you crashed to the ground.

Scared stiff I shouldered you
trembling, across coarse land
to seek help from tried minds.
Today my heart skips with joy
pressing love to my gaunt breast.
Today my mind jogs with pride
crooning songs of the mind's mind,

songs to give the kiss of life
to those who sustain bruises
digging to plant new history,
songs to make genuine farmers
break ground in the right season.
Let it rain and rain today
that throats dry as a dog's bone
may sing the harshness of drought
and the tyranny of fear.

COUNTING ON YOU 1

Doubt came down on me
like a thief at night,
hammered my mind blank
and drove me to doubt.
Dumb doubt came down on me
like a wall not well built,
fastened the door of thought
and showed me the way out.
I screamed in gruesome pain
like a he-goat at castration
till the sympathy in your eyes
whipped up in me the desire
to hang on, even in tatters.

The days rolled on swiftly
like rainy season streams.
I saw the world take wing
resolved to change clothing.
Blind Ambition, visibly moved
urged me to take another look
at how my lantern is burning.
Then I turned after wasted years
to where you often lay musing,
wondering why life is so harsh.
I beheld new hope in your eyes.
Though the season was bellicose
I bound myself to live through it
to finish first in the rough race
to secure a seat in your heart
singing new songs from my mind's mind.

COUNTING ON YOU 11

I must acknowledge dear
that never before now
have I lost so much blood
struggling to stitch the shreds
of my hard to grasp life.
Never before sweet soul
have I given attention
to the doom in the offing
dogging every crooked mind.
I bank on you to sail through
the bumpy road to success.

Now that I hold your hand
firm in mine hard as rock
I know down to the ground
that my loss of balance
would never ever again
be one that would destroy me.
I have found a restful place
where I can lie without fear
and sleep when it is stormy.
I count on you to drink joy
and juice from your strawberries.

God has raised us with kids,
five heartwarming issues
looking up to us dear
for shelter from wild minds.
I am awake to love

and of a mind like you
to care for the children
plunging a sharp-edged knife
into the womb of self.
I know it is a battle
fierce and fraught with anxiety
but I count on you my rose
to stand with me in sandstorms.
I count on you my darling
to groom the youngsters in love
in a world of moral rot.

OVERLOADED HEART

I am worried, even as you
who yawn but never hit the hay.
My heart chafes in expectation
like yours but without assistance.
I too drive pigs to the market
but my muscles hardly wear down
pushing low life away from us.
If I should die without steeling
the hearts that shall sorrow for me,
forget not to make the world know
I sang about love, greed and truth,
my miffed mind in the combat zone.

I have no second thoughts like you
who dream but never reap the fruits.
My songs stare people in the face
like yours but without tenderness.
I too dream like every artist
but my dreams hardly carry me
away from the sharks amidst us.
If I should wither without words,
tell the world how I cherished peace,
how I sang about mad cravings
and wished Cameroon were starlit
with minds ready to root out graft.

I am worried, even as you
who stargaze but never garner.
My mind roams overcast, sweating

like yours seeking the Beautiful.
I have no silver tongue like you
but my music never gives up
caressing the strings of false hearts.
Let not my endeavour be drowned
if I should wilt without slaying
the foul spirit that shakes us lame.
I sing about bad blood and death,
my mind ready to die for Truth.

DEEP CARE

Although the shock still lingers
hot in the belly of Love
here on this dismal dry land
with neither flowers nor mouths
to freshen and buck us up,
I care not whether you laugh
or cry when I end this song.
Day after day my hungry heart
does a strange sanguinary dance
torn by the claws of injustice.
I care deeply about the man
sitting close to you without clothes.

The way I embrace the world
since my eyes wolfed your beauty
and my heart drooled over you
makes a thousand foolish mouths
allege I have a bird's brains.
I care not whether you scream
or dance when I beat my drums.
From time to time my bruised ego
picks up a quarrel with the world
fed up with treacherous soulmates.
I care much about the woman
labouring near you without drugs.

Although my word of honour
given in the heart of glee
in the presence of the moon

stirred up questions in your mind
and rivals sang dampening songs,
you never ever shut me out.
Nights of rude storms or days of grief
may still propel you towards fear,
the beast we must bring to its knees
to move forward and shine like stars.
I have taken an oath, my love
never to close the door to your views.
I care with rare passion about you
spending your time without full focus.
I cannot allow my greedy mind
deceive you with groundless promises.

FUWAM THE PROFESSOR 1

Fuwam my once close friend
now just a mere shadow.
You need a sledge hammer
to hammer your stale thoughts
till they faint and fade out
for the crowd to trust you.
The masses on their knees
need true and decent minds
to lift them out of the trance
that has made them lose sight of
the weighty issues of thumbs down
and the wreckage of our riches.

You need a few repairs
at knifepoint professor
to view the world clearly.
Why should you, born to fly
and soar like an eagle
rub your nose in the dirt
only to carry begging bowls
to put some life into your eyes?
The world around you wonders why
you who were very dear to them
should turn around and savage them
thinking only of your rank paunch.
Real men and women wonder why
you who used to be so upright
should change hue like a chameleon
thinking only of your own bread.

FUWAM THE PROFESSOR 11

I feel sad for you Fuwam.
You were one in a million,
one with whom I could commune
and share the dreams I cherish
seated by some babbling brook
to bring to mind the blossoms
that no longer bloom in this land.

Life without light without truth
can bring many to their knees
and drive them to unripe death.
I stuck to you like a shadow
hoping to blow quack lecturers
away from every lecture hall
with our cantankerous numbers.
But you purposed to board the train
that drives intellectuals to sleep.

You vented your spleen on light,
shut candour in a dark room
and offered your soul to sharks.
I won't call you an enemy
so let me sing without collars
till the excrement in your blood
hits the arrogance in your voice.
Let me sing without cutting back
till the poison in your system
drives you to unalloyed healers.
I understand you sing your songs

without strain and tears for favours.
Whatever the case, let us close ranks
and show the ignorant the right way.
Let us join forces with the masses
and fight injustice Fuwam the prof.

FUWAM THE PROFESSOR 111

Dance on in your arrogance
countryman without standards
to the jagged music of graft.
Let not my impudent thoughts
nor these stark naked verses
invite a cut-throat squabble.
May my love for winsome minds
turn your kingdom upside down.

Dance on in your sauciness
professor with no treatise
to the music of small minds.
Let not my impudent tongue
nor the punches of my pen
leave the door open for war.
May my fervour for finesse
break the rocks of your folly.

Dance on in your gracelessness
man of letters with no wreath.
Charging thunderstorms gather
to relieve the land of trash
and set the pace for rebirth.
I see just time in the wind
calm but sure to untie knots.
What dance shall you dance professor
when the dawn of clean hands breaks?
What yarn shall you spin lecturer
when Nemesis calls for your head

without hair without insurance?

You make me jump out of my skin
professor with nothing in print.
What kind of music shall you sing
when you go to meet your forebears?
What kind of headgear shall you wear
when you stand before them tongue-tied?
Show me well-read man of letters
the mask you shall don on that day.
I hear you teach your students that
flowers can grow on plots of stone.
The strong as steel talons of time
will someday sink into your flesh.

LITTLE UFONG 1

I saw her clearly
little dark Ufong
alone in the dark,
quaking in the cold
like a rainsoaked chick
her dreams on the rocks.

An army of children
gathered to needle her
crawled away in laughter.
Men battered by beer sneered
and night women in white
wept out their lustful lungs.

Little Ufong eyed them
like a trapped rat a cat.
Alone she spoke and sighed
and sang a song with tears.
Draw near and see for yourselves
the flint heart of a mother.
Draw near and hear Ufong sing
the song of her heartsick life.
Draw near and see for yourselves
the bad blood of a father.
My hard to win over heart
goes out to little Ufong.

Her swarthy pretty face
and twinkling eyes of blue

can take your breath away
and move your mind to weep.
My eyes were wide in wonder
as I stared in awed silence
the pleasing to the eye bird.
I doubt if her parents breathe.
The breath of air moans and groans
as Ufong grasps all her strength,
lets out a groan of toothed pain
and worms her way towards chance.

LITTLE UFONG 11

She wears her sadness still,
pretty star-crossed Ufong
by herself in the streets,
hopeful someone would help.
She wraps her soiled loincloth
around the neck of Hope
and waits for crumbs of love.

It was after the rains,
the sun had just risen.
I was bound for my den
to run through a new song
when she reeled towards me.
She was not liquored up,
pretty ill-starred Ufong.

Waves of weighty feelings
washed through me like sea surf.
Second thoughts drained my blood
and an awesome feeling
gripped me as I watched her,
ripping tears in my heart.
There was want in her eyes
but she was first class still,
the beauty but the jinxed
I beheld in the dark
frightened out of her wits
many many moons back.
She wants to find her roots

though the journey is miles.

I have searched, thinking twice
through my piqued mind for room
to keep her far from pests,
broken smiles and laughter.
I have promised myself
there will be no more funk
to make peace with my heart
hopeful she finds her roots.
I will climb hills with her
and feed her famished heart
with viands, candour and love.
I will keep her company
till a propitious wind blows
and tidies the stage for her.

TAKE BACK YOUR LOVE

You blew open my love
behind the pit latrine
you dug beside your heart
and dragged me to the tree
where many dimwits have perished,
daggers of misplaced resentment
dangling from their assaulted breasts.
Give me back my deep-rooted love
so I can sing away knife thoughts.

You bloated my love with whisky
in the mansion of tainted glass
you built in the kernel of town
but offered me hemlock as toast
at the foot of the tree of death,
I whose lips and love ignited
in your hard-bitten heart the flames
which today reduce to mere ash
the branches that led you to plums.

I stood by the tree of death
and wept tears of frustration,
watching my fort of love tumble.
The black blinds of the evening
and the crimson claws of vultures
set my afflicted heart pounding.
If this be the path cleared for me
in the mangrove forest of life
then let me no longer complain

nor beat the tom-tom of failure.
If this be the way I must take
to win the prize I languish for
then let me no longer labour.
Let me kiss your powdered pale cheeks,
I who dragged your love across streets
teeming with lies and nakedness.
Take back your bred in the bone love
but let me nurse your wounded heart.

TREACHEROUS ARROW

You do not feel traitor,
the bites and the itches
plus the tension within
in this dry-eyed region
where men rival mosquitoes
and women compete with fleas
for crumbs of the public cake.
I hurl defiance at you rogue
with the virulence of vipers
and the deadly sting of scorpions.

You stand accused trickster.
You wheedled me here bound
like an ill-disposed goat.
I hurl defiance at you,
you who smuggled my chickens
to feed fat your viciousness.
I double my fists traitor
and multiply my verbal kicks
for the whole world to understand
you do not know the way to love.

Today under your boots
we groan, my whole household
struggling to lift our eyes
to drink the beauty of stars
and sniff at flowers unbound
like butterflies and swallows.
Lay out your life as you want

laced with methadone and gin
but let me and my offspring
plant and harvest our efforts.
If the small voice is stilled
the nation will come to grief.
If true-born love is strangled
and thrown into dustbin bags
we will not stand storming storms.
I hurl defiance at you wretch
on crack assignment for the poor.
I hurl defiance at you bat,
treacherous arrow in my heart.

EARNEST APPEAL

I caught my harassing heart
strolling blue last evening
by the simple graves of hearts
who yesterday did not allow
hatred wrap its lethal hands
around the neck of our land.
They shall no longer take joy
in the passionate prolonged war
between what was but is no more
and the doom that looms over us,
the rank and file that championed love
while hate axed heads in broad daylight.

Come down fellow countrymen
from the mount of rooting out
to the plains of production
where in composed reflection
side by side with the masses,
we can a fresh vision weave
around the necks of young heads.
Let all dynamic minds gather
in the grandstand of construction
to give hope to frustrated souls
and smooth Beauty's ruffled feathers
for Love and Truth to wear their crowns
as we consciously stitch our hearts
to squash hand-to-mouth existence.
Come down from your mount of intrigues
so we can flatten hills of rift

and cultivate a caring image.

Our kids have to have cover
to shoot up sure of themselves,
free from doubt and fickleness.
We have to stick out our necks
for them to make a breakthrough
in a world so fierce so bleak.
We have to show them the road
and plead with tyrannical life
to be gentle with their visions.

Come disillusioned kith and kin
so we can mend our broken shields
and clear the way for the children.

I LOVE WHISTLING

I love whistling at night
when the moon is well-rounded,
when crickets have had their bath
and nightbirds alight dead drunk
on some rooftops to snuff out
the candles of callous minds.

I saw the light of day here
to bear with polished courage
my ordeals and the sandstorms
that send many to their graves
before the gathering season.
I will thence stick like a limpet
to the rocks of my toilsome craft
serene in a breeezy and cool night,
whistling reposefully to myself.

I love to chuckle at dawn
when the eyeball of heaven
peeps out from behind the hills
and sparrows twitter and squawk
in the trees, entreating man
to awake and brave another day.
During darksome and stormy seasons
I too stumble and topple headlong
over boulders and broken bottles
like a house in a state of decay.
At such thorny and cutting moments
anger rises like yeast to slaughter

not only the myriad beasts of prey
but also souls that shame the nation.
Whistling lessens the cramps of anger.

I love to whistle at night
when the moon is conspicuous,
when the breath of wind whistles
and moths wing against windows
calling to mind the dry night
I first heard about my Love.

BREATHING STILL

Somehow we continue to breathe
since your mysterious departure.
I remember how in darkness
we strove to liberate our minds
from the ferrous prison of fear.
Sometimes I felt my blood run cold
as I held out in the darkness
a lantern of love and lineage
to brighten our way to freedom
and point us to new ways of life.

We continue to breathe kinsman
since your mindboggling betrayal.
I still remember how in light
we strained every nerve to make sure
our people break bread with Truth
without falling prey to strangers.
Sometimes I shook like a jelly
as I struggled in the darkness
to sing a song to cheer us up
and prepare the groundwork for change.

Somehow we continue to breathe
since you deserted us for loot.
Alone we put together songs
sprinkled with our people's history
which today groans in grinding pain
under the boots of Western lords
and the spikes of Oriental gods.

My arms are still set to embrace
those who opted out of the scheme
to build around our raw materials
before embracing foreign counsel.
My mind is predisposed to welcome
those willing to redeem the nation.
I see a sweet and sunny season
spreading her arresting aroma
rapidly, through the entire nation,
filling every mind with useful concepts.
I see young people sprouting like mushroom
spreading steadily across the country.
I see them straightening out our history.

STILL SMALL VOICE

I have longed for the day
when we shall break the ice
and give love the glad eye
to knock our nation into shape.
I have hankered after the day
when we shall throw off dependence
and move away from sterile land
to hammer out a new nation
and show the world our competence.
My still small voice loves liberty
and my mind relishes strain songs.

I have longed to clean out
the junk in your thinking
but fear some silly tongues
might lash you into dead silence
and convince some lowbrow pundits
to tear to shreds self-assertion.
I have no choice but storm against
the rallying growls of highbrows
scrambling like wards for royal robes.
Though I sometimes freeze with horror
watching terror grow more monstrous,
I cannot stop my still small voice
from putting into words the songs
that will stir up every household
for the world to see our seriousness.

I still long for the day

when we shall chat as one
and send to the gallows
the traitors that tarnish our pride.
I still hunger after that day
when we shall get rid of thraldom
and establish a just strong state
to show the world we too can build
and change the history of the world.
My still small voice loves fair treatment
and scope for each and every mind.

THEY WILL RISE

I see them rising
like the morning sun,
the children we nursed
armed not with slogans
but with bills that clip
the wings of wild birds.
I see them marching
like black soldier ants
filled not with compromise
but with the firm resolve
to weed out corrupt souls.
The time may seem far off
the waiting mind-numbing
but they will surely rise,
the children from our loins
to give back our dignity.

The fear of miscarriage
may make your blood run cold.
The claws of death may shake
grey, the last leaves of hope
on the tree in your heart.
I see blooms high and low
and our tears drying off.
The scars we have carried
this long, groaning in darkness
will heal in the wet season
when the pedlars of death crash.
The beauty of this rich land

floating in the sea of slime
will shine once more my people
when the children from our loins
clear the land of piggish statesmen.

FIND YOUR FEET AGAIN

The land surrounding you
near the neck of the woods
makes my surly soul swell
not because of its charm
but because of the flowers
blooming in your sunlit eyes.

The stillness in the place
makes me bedeck my thoughts
thinking hard through the night
not because of your calls
but because of the soft spot
I have for this cracked country.

Torn hearts infest the place
bemoaning through the night
the loss of their sweethearts
nursing hope to love once more.
The flourishing leeks in bloom
and the bracing sparkling brooks
spark hope in the disheartened,
those who fought for a just state.

Your heartache will shrivel
and your foes will shiver
when they learn you blossom.
Come then with me stricken soul
into these woods of green shoots
to find your feet once again.

The Stygian gloom in your eyes
will grow into tameless flames.

BEYOND BELIEF

We are a community
full of overweening pride.
Our tongues are sharp as razors
our hearts the home of sham love.
We are at each other's throat
like visionless wayward subjects
determined to batter their land
for morsels of beef and cookies.
We are beyond belief people
tearing our hearts for alien feed.

We are a bizarre people
thriving on lies and gossip.
No one unsheathes affection
for the country raped and sick.
We have become ruthless foes
bent on dealing faithlessly
with the dreams we babysat
before lame liberty came.
Rash politicians use us
day by day like toilet tissue
while hit and miss intellectuals
burn the midnight oil concocting
information that numbs the mind.
I will not cease undressing you
till you seize control of treason
and the nation wakes from slumber.
We are beyond belief creatures,
a tongue-in-cheek community

willing like a fresh loose woman
to sell our consciences for cash.

My distress runs very deep,
my tears flow from a heart rent
and dragged in the mud always.
I do not weep blind brothers
over private woes and lose.
I weep because we are obtuse,
self-indulgent and black-hearted.
I weep because fallen angels
snatch our teenagers and smash them
against concrete walls while we cheer.

KATAKATA

They call him Katakata,
people very close to him
not because he has no name
nor because he is lawless
but because he resents wrong.
He is the kind of wordsmith
with a heart for his calling
so he leaves no stone unturned
to make his customers pleased.
He labours with no stretch out
like honeybees in season.
He sleeps with complaining mice
and swallows insults daily
for his consumers and friends
to live well in all seasons.

They call him Katakata,
people faraway from him
not because he causes trouble
nor because he is hard up
but because he amazes them.
He is the kind of craftsman
with a heart for what is right
so he works himself to death
to brush his people's history.
He longs for the hand of love
and curses dignity in green
to secure the hand of love
and make his countrymen see

the need to set store by love.
We need love to beat the world.

You call him Katakata
not because you dislike him
nor because he is all ears,
turning inside out your lives
but because he lynches lies.
He is the kind of artist
with a heart for his people
so he journeys through the land
to give hope to his backers.
Strangers have invaded us,
sundered the love that linked us
and given love new meaning.
It makes no sense countrymen
to seed seeds of belonging
so vital, bracing and close
to reap but revolting fruits.
It makes no sense prime movers
to produce works soaked in black lore
so precious, pregnant and priceless
to stoop but to white traditions.

I call him Katakata
not because he pipes strange songs
but because he loves the truth.
He beats the drum with vigour
like those who came before him,
those who sang their people's lives
and danced away their hatred

sharing palm wine and kola
under the palaver tree.
We need Katakata's mind
to beat shame and ignorance.
We need Katakata's mind
to rekindle our old ways
and soar above intruders.
We need a sense of purpose
to whip ourselves into shape
to shape up our shun country
coming apart at the seams,
impoverished year by year
by corrupt public servants.

TURN LOOSE THE BEAST

Innocent birds lament still
fluttering through unsafe space
since their homes were demolished.
Those who torment them rejoice,
dancing dauntless in the dark
but in the light they take flight.
Such a strange strain of actors
shall someday set our homes ablaze
save we turn loose the beast in us
to flagellate to death the beasts
that have for years abused our love.

I want to break cola nuts
daily with the homeless birds
singing songs that spur the mind
to break the link with boot boys
breaking the back of the poor.
The dog-eared life of these birds
stares every soul in the face
like the light of morn at sunrise
yet many hearts green with envy
throw stones and shout insults at them.
I want to break kola with them.

Though their plight descends heavy
on my breast like a millstone,
I will not throw stones at them
nor fill their minds with mad thoughts.
I will guide them to unknown trees

and show them where to reconstruct.
I will stand by them even though
the punches of the night are hard,
bringing to mind the fate man shares
with beasts in a land ruled by brutes.
The thorny thoughts of yesterday,
fierce as a bear robbed of her cubs
locked in battle with wolly thoughts,
remind me of the endless strife
between straight and crooked thinkers.
I will follow the course of light
and enjoy the smell of flowers
but turn loose the beast inside me
when darkness lays claim to my head.
Turn loose the beast in you soulmate
when dogs attempt to tear your flesh
and politicians switch your brains.

INTRANSIGENT FISTS

Pettiness with bigotry
line the streets with perjury
and wrap their jagged tentacles
round the souls of the gullible
to flood the nation with falsehood.
Even those born just yesterday
galloping on their breasts, sweating
with strong perfume in their voices
seek to join the chorus of guile,
the deadly serpent in man's heart.

I have now grasped very well
the emotions of the heart.
I can now without stalling
get to the bottom of the war
raging between mediocre minds
and souls groomed for stupendous feats.
I must therefore sing wholehearted,
songs that sterilize the senses
and steer people toward stardom.
You too can either beat deep drums
or while away your time on booze
depriving your household of bread.

Though before balding big guns
I kneel in contempt of psyche
and beseech highbrows to shine,
I know nothing fruitful will bud.
The intransigent fists of time

will break the neck of perjury
and gouge out the eyes of bungling.
Burgeoning tongues of candidness
will new life breathe into zombies
and leave the browbeaten, the stage
to present their brand of freedom.
I wish I could breathe until then
to feel the freshness of fair play
and speak the language of power.
I wish I could witness the fall,
the death of those milking the land.

DANCE OF THE END

I have no time for fools
and no home for turncoats.
Their running with the hare
and hunting with the hounds
has left a deep deep wound
in a mind that did care
and gave them well cooked food.

Let them stick to their trade
going for large lush deals.
The fiction in their throats
and the guile in their eyes
brewed in mills in the West
cascade down every street.
Let them have their field day
singing Janus-faced hymns
for their stomachs and flesh.
They should take their last steps
and drink till they get drunk
in the dance of the end
with neither tambourines
nor songs of the mind's mind.

I am audible in my beats
and frank about our quandary.
We need a dry season fire
to sweep across the whole nation
till the corruption in our blood
and the greed in our conscience die

leaving no room for listless minds.

I see resentment in your eyes
leaping up and down in anger,
unable to stomach my thrust.
You like working with simple souls
stripped naked of their perception
to stitch your file for promotion.
You can bring comfort to your ears
singing in the land of sleep songs
for people like you without dreams.
Sing your last treacherous songs mugs
and drink the most leading champagne
in the looming dance of the end
with neither tears and compunction
nor sighs to lead you to the grave.

www.ingramcontent.com/pod-product-compliance
Lightning Source LLC
Chambersburg PA
CBHW022107160426
43198CB00008B/390